Let my heart be broken by the things that break the heart of God.

DR. ROBERT PIERCE, *founder of World Vision*

World Vision

Building a better world for children

"We always thank God for all of you . . .

We continually remember . . .

your work produced by faith,

your labor prompted by love,

and your endurance inspired

by hope in our Lord Jesus Christ."

I THESSALONIANS 1:2-3

PRESENTED TO _____

PRESENTED BY _____

ON _____

World Vision

our faith in action

"Let my heart be broken by the things that break the heart of God."

BOB PIERCE, FOUNDER, WORLD VISION

"For God so loved the world that he gave his one and only Son…" JOHN 3:16

Dear Friend:

I believe the key verse in all of Scripture is John 3:16. In one sentence, the expansive Judeo-Christian history is given meaning, the love of a proactive God is unfurled, and a startling future hope—free to all who believe—is revealed. God did not stand at a distance, idly observing a world broken by sin. He reached out to humankind, and, at great personal expense, offered new life to all who would believe.

The Bible is God's love letter to the world and, ultimately, it is a call to action for those who have received His gift. A call to love others in the same manner that God has loved us—actively and unconditionally. A call to care for the orphans and widows, to pursue justice, to extend the hand of mercy.

This unique study Bible brings these critical aspects of faith into sharp focus—to breathe new life into what it means to put our faith into action and become salt and light in the world.

The message of the Bible remains absolutely relevant and critical. The message is love. And our response is obedience. In Jesus' words, the fullest expression of our love can be dealt and felt in something as simple as giving a thirsty child a cup of cold water.

For more than 50 years, World Vision has provided ways for Christians all over the world to put their faith into action. We pray that the photos and verses on the following pages will inspire you to see the world through God's eyes, and love others in the same manner that He has loved us.

Sincerely,

Richard Stearns
President
World Vision, United States office

"'Here am I. Send me!'" ISAIAH 6:8

Dr. Robert Pierce, founder of World Vision

As a young man, Bob Pierce answered the calling he felt to preach the gospel. But during a trip to China in 1947, he discovered that his listeners needed more than words to understand and respond to God's love. He saw that the power of the gospel was demonstrated in the actions of those who fed, clothed, and cared for the hurting.

After sharing the gospel with Chinese schoolchildren on the island of Amoy (now Xiamen), Bob discovered that one of his young listeners—a girl named White Jade—had received Christ only to be cast out by her family. A local missionary challenged Bob to support White Jade with food and clothing, and money for school. He offered five dollars— all he had in his pocket—and promised to send more each month.

That singular act of compassion—one person reaching out to one child in need—is still at the heart of World Vision. Since 1950, the year Bob Pierce founded World Vision, millions of people the world over have acted in faith to make a difference, one child at a time.

Top right Bob Pierce often prayed, "Let my heart be broken by the things that break the heart of God."
Bottom left and right Bob Pierce with orphaned boys and girls.

"He who has compassion on them will guide them and lead them beside springs of water." ISAIAH 49:10

Water is life

Sofia (left), from Villcapujio, Bolivia, smiles as she pumps fresh water from a new well located just a few steps from her family's home. In many thirsty, desolate communities, bleak life-expectancy rates have etched an oft-spoken adage—"water is life"—deep into the community's consciousness. More than I billion people do not have access to clean, safe water. Their only alternative is to drink from dirty, disease-infested water sources. Jesus often used water as an illustration of life, and he spoke of the impact made by providing even one cup of cold water. When a community gains access to safe water, its children's chances of survival immediately double and the outlook of the entire community is transformed.

Opposite bottom left Aynura, 8, collects water for washing from a garbage dump in Imishli, Azerbaijan.
Opposite bottom right A traditional shallow well in Sri Lanka is dry due to drought.
Top right A child in Ghana risks his life to gather dirty water from a pond that is home to several crocodiles.
Right Water gushes from a new well in the Philippines.

"For I was hungry and you gave me something to eat." MATTHEW 25:35

Nourish the hungry

Eight-year-old Tantine (lower right), drinks therapeutic milk at a World Vision feeding center in the Democratic Republic of Congo. The center feeds children like Tantine from families who have either been displaced or are unable to grow their own food as a result of years of civil war that have ravaged this central African country. World Vision also supplies antibiotics, de-worming medications, and immunizations. When Jesus said, "I was hungry and you gave me something to eat," He was speaking on behalf of the poor and hungry throughout all generations. Giving something as simple as a warm meal to someone in need is a tangible expression of our love for Christ.

Bottom left Orphans in Malawi enjoy a nourishing breakfast.
Top right Families begin to stir after spending a cold night outside in Ethiopia during the great famine of the mid-1980s.

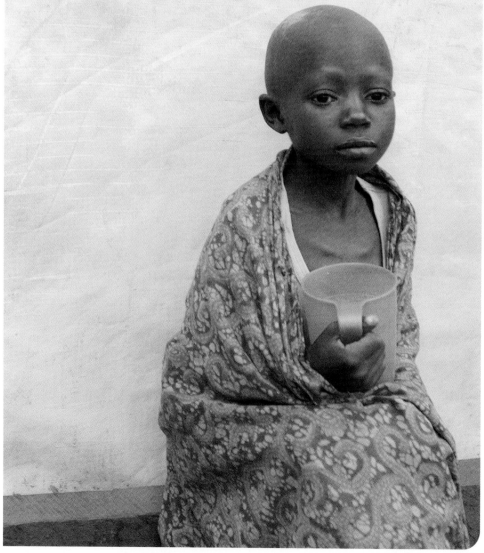

The joy of child sponsorship

Jesus loves children. And He calls us to welcome children like He does. More than 2 million people around the world have welcomed children into their hearts through World Vision child sponsorship. The connection a child feels to their sponsor is a constant reminder of God's love. And it makes a child feel special. He or she receives access to basic needs like nutritious food, clean water, an education, health care, and more. And a sponsor feels the joy of knowing that their open arms are welcoming more than a child—they are welcoming Christ Himself.

Above Sponsored boys in Haiti.
Opposite top left A sponsor meets her Ghanaian sponsored child for the first time.
Opposite top right A sponsored child from El Salvador treasures the photos and gifts she has received from her American sponsor.
Right Sponsorship helps children realize their full, God-given potential.

"And whoever welcomes a little child like this in my name welcomes me."

MATTHEW 18:5

"Yet I am poor and needy;
come quickly to me, O God." PSALM 70:5

When disaster strikes

It only takes a few seconds for a person to lose everything. Earthquakes, floods, civil conflicts, and other disasters mercilessly reduce a person's existence to what they need to survive: food, water, and shelter. It is in one's moment of greatest need that help often arrives. God describes Himself as an ever-present help in times of trouble; He rescues the desperate and gives strength to the weary. But He doesn't work alone. He calls on His people to join in the thrilling, privileged task of acting as His hands and feet, reaching those in need. World Vision participated in such a moment in 1978 on the South China Sea when the Seasweep vessel rescued the cousin of a crew member (right), just one of hundreds of refugees who were adrift and dying on the open sea.

Below Survival kits, food, and seeds arrive for flood victims in Mozambique, 2000.
Opposite top left Bangladesh, 2004
Opposite top right World Vision staff and locals help evacuate an elderly woman during floods in the Dominican Republic.

"Let your light shine before men, that they may see your good deeds and praise your Father in heaven." MATTHEW 5:16

When light shines

Poverty of the spirit can be the most miserable poverty of all. A life empty of hope is not made full by food, clean water, or medical care. But acts of mercy that meet needs such as these open one's heart to receive God's promise of abundant life and eternal hope. Whether we are digging a well, feeding the hungry, or strengthening a local church, everything we do is motivated by our faith in Jesus Christ and our desire to show God's unconditional love to all people.

"Defend the cause of the weak and fatherless; maintain the rights of the poor and oppressed." PSALM 82:3

Top left Orphans in Romania, 1991
Top right Abandoned or orphaned children living on the streets of Yangon, Myanmar, receive shelter, food, health care, and education at World Vision's drop-in center.
Bottom right Desperately poor children sort through garbage in Calcutta, India.

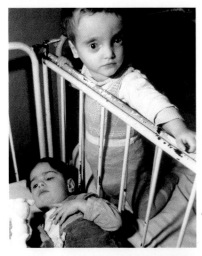

Too young to be on their own

Millions of children around the world live without any adult care. Many have been orphaned; others abandoned or sold; some abducted and abused. All desperately need to be connected to even just one person who can ensure their basic needs are met and remind them that they are loved. They also need advocates who will speak on their behalf, maintain their rights, and protect them from exploitation and oppression.

"'Whatever you did for one of the least of these… you did for me.'" MATTHEW 25:40

Disabled, but not defeated

At just 9 years old, Anuka's legs are badly bent by rickets (right). One in three Mongolian children is stricken with this bone disease caused by vitamin D deficiency. While the chances of a full recovery for Anuka are slim due to her age and the severity of her illness, rickets can be healed if treated early enough. It also can be prevented with nutritional supplements. Jesus identified Himself with children like Anuka who suffer from disabilities and physical deformities when He said, "'… whatever you did for one of the least of these … you did for me.'" Some World Vision donors have said that when they look into the eyes of a community's "throw-away" children, they see the face of Jesus.

Left A young girl at the Crippled Children's Home, Bangladesh, 1975.
Opposite bottom left Darfur, Sudan, 2004
Opposite bottom right Both of Vikas' legs were crushed during a massive earthquake that struck India in 2001. World Vision staff, moved by his condition, gave of their own resources to pay for corrective surgeries and prosthetics for his legs.

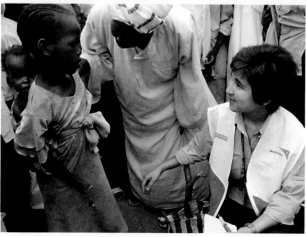

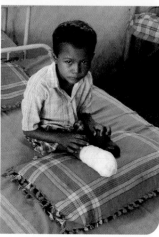

HIV/AIDS: a generation of orphans and widows

Both of Khadija's grown daughters have died of AIDS-related illnesses, leaving 2-year-old Kidoki (below left) and four other orphaned children in her care. The family's only income is the $12 a month the oldest child earns as a maid. The HIV/AIDS crisis has created millions of orphans and widows. God's Word is very clear about His heart for orphans and widows. It's no surprise that James says our care for them is one of the purest expressions of our faith.

Opposite top left More than 15 million children around the world have been orphaned by AIDS.
Opposite top right Since her mother's death, 8-year-old Skala has taken over the care of her baby sister, Hope.
Top A Rwandan woman—pregnant and now infected with the AIDS virus.
Bottom In Cambodia, World Vision helps reduce the misunderstanding, fear, and discrimination that traditionally surround HIV/AIDS.

"Religion that God our Father accepts as pure and faultless is this: to look after orphans and widows in their distress…" JAMES 1:27

"Blessed are the peacemakers." MATTHEW 5:9

Standing up for peace

Like most Colombians caught in their country's deadly crossfire between gang warfare, drug trafficking, and military extremists, Mayerly Sanchez (opposite, shown here at age 14) desperately desires peace. But Mayerly, a former sponsored child, has taken decisive action. She co-led a national children's peace movement that was nominated for the 1998 Nobel Peace Prize. "We define peace in four words," she says. "Love, acceptance, forgiveness, and work."

Top Ugandan children who were once abducted by rebel soldiers demonstrate a peace chain.
Bottom A survivor of the Rwandan genocide, 1994.

"If there is a poor man among you...do not be...tightfisted.

Living generously

It is the dedication of donors like Kelly Minter (below) that makes World Vision's work possible. Around the world, millions of compassionate people live their lives in openhandedness toward the poor. Their genuine faith finds expression through their generosity; their gifts are a sacred offering to God. For this reason, World Vision practices the highest standards of stewardship, taking "pains to do what is right, not only in the eyes of the Lord but also in the eyes of men" (2 Corinthians 8:21).

...Rather be openhanded and freely lend him whatever he needs." DEUTERONOMY 15:7-8

Top left 30 Hour Famine participants in Tanzania.
Top center An immunization is prepared for a baby in Mauritania.
Top right Families in Cambodia take orphaned children in as their own.

"Let us not love with words or tongue but with actions and in truth." I JOHN 3:18

Faith in action

When World Vision is at its best, it is simply a bridge between the materially rich and those with very little. For more than 50 years, World Vision has had the privilege of helping millions of compassionate people cross the bridge to help those in need. As people put their faith into action, their own lives are transformed. They see hope shining in the eyes of children, mothers, and fathers. And the wonderful irony of Christ's words awes their hearts: "'It is more blessed to give than to receive'" (Acts 20:35).

Below The authenticity of a World Vision worker's love is felt by an orphaned boy.
Opposite One man's faith in action sees a frightened young boy across floodwaters in the Dominican Republic.
Opposite bottom left Tai Anderson, of the band Third Day, dances with children from Lesotho.
Opposite bottom right Children in Chicago receive tangible help.

" 'I have come that they may have life, and have it to the full.' " JOHN 10:10

"Whoever heard me spoke well of me . . .

because I rescued the poor who cried for help,

and the fatherless who had none to assist him.

The man who was dying blessed me;

I made the widow's heart sing.

I put on righteousness as my clothing;

justice was my robe and my turban.

I was eyes to the blind and feet to the lame.

I was a father to the needy;

I took up the case of the stranger."

Job 29:11-16